PLAGUES
The Microscopic Battlefield

PLAGUES
The Microscopic Battlefield

FALYNN KOCH

:01

First Second

New York

First Second

Penciled with a light blue Staedtler Triplus Fineliner and Manga Studio.
Inked with a Maru-style digital nib and colored digitally in Photoshop.
Lettered with the Comicrazy font from Comicraft.

Published by First Second
First Second is an imprint of Roaring Brook Press,
a division of Holtzbrinck Publishing Holdings Limited Partnership
120 Broadway, New York, NY 10271
All rights reserved

Library of Congress Control Number: 2016945566

Paperback ISBN 978-1-62672-752-6
Hardcover ISBN 978-1-62672-753-3

Our books may be purchased in bulk for promotional, educational, or business use. Please
contact your local bookseller or the Macmillan Corporate and Premium Sales Department
at (800) 221-7945 ext. 5442 or by e-mail at MacmillanSpecialMarkets@macmillan.com.

First edition 2017
Series editor: Dave Roman
Plagues consultant: Dorothy H. Crawford
Book design by John Green

Printed in China by Toppan Leefung Printing Ltd., Dongguan City, Guangdong Province
Paperback: 10
Hardcover: 10 9 8 7 6 5

"A plague o' both your houses!"

—William Shakespeare, *Romeo and Juliet*

We live in a world teeming with microorganisms, creatures that go back to the very beginnings of our world, if not before. Long after we have vanished as a species and all evidence of our civilization has turned to dust, bacteria and viruses will still be here.

For over a decade, the Canadian poet and self-taught geneticist Christian Bök has been trying to weave a poem into the genome of *Deinococcus radiodurans*, a bacterium so tough it can survive the vacuum of outer space and the intense radiation of a nuclear reactor without mutating. If successful, Bök's poem, *The Xenotext*, will become an integral part of *Deinococcus radiodurans*'s genetic code. Millions of years from now, some advanced species may crack that code, read Bök's poem, and know that once upon a time we were here. It's even possible, as astrophysicist Paul Davies has suggested, that some now-extinct civilization in a solar system far, far away may have already tried this form of interstellar texting. If only we had the right app, some of the viruses and bacteria with whom we share our world—perhaps even some that make us sick, like yellow fever or the bubonic plague—may turn out to have arrived here long ago with a mission to endlessly replicate an eternal message: we exist, we exist, we exist.

I had the good luck to be born in Southern California after the invention of the polio vaccine, only a few years before the eradication of smallpox. The US Public Health Service ensured I was vaccinated against those diseases as well as measles, diphtheria, whooping cough, and other historical scourges of childhood. I had access to antibiotics in an era before there was much antibiotic resistance. When I got sick, science helped me get well. So in junior high, when I read *A Distant Mirror: The Calamitous 14th Century*, Barbara Tuchman's riveting account of the late Middle Ages, her chapter on the Black Death blew my mind. The idea of an epidemic that could kill tens of millions of people in a span of years seemed like science fiction, a zombie apocalypse that actually happened. Tuchman's book sparked my lifelong fascination with science and history. When I chose illustration for a career, I gravitated toward clients like *National Geographic*, *Scientific American*, and NASA. When I finally started writing and illustrating my own books for kids, I focused on disasters, epidemics, climate change, and the West's deep debt to the scientific culture of the medieval Muslim world. The opening chapter of my own book about plagues, *Outbreak*, focuses on the Black Death.

Before Louis Pasteur proved the germ theory of disease, we blamed plagues not on bacteria and viruses but on God, Satan, evil spirits, and bad smells. We especially blamed the powerless: hated ethnic groups, outsiders, uppity women, and people who looked different, talked different, or believed different than we did. We ostracized them, murdered them, then stole their property. Eventually the plague would burn itself out. Killing everyone it could kill, the disease would die out until new susceptible victims were born. Then it would return. Locals would say, "People wearing red hats moved into our village, and then smallpox came to our village. We killed all the red hat people and smallpox stopped. Therefore, the red hat people caused smallpox." This is the classic logical error of *post hoc ergo proctor hoc*. Because this event follows that event, this event must have been *caused* by that event.

When it comes to infectious disease, human beings are still susceptible to this kind of false logic. Homosexuals were blamed and persecuted during the early years of the AIDS epidemic as the cause of the disease; public health workers were attacked for the same reasons during the Ebola crisis; terrified conspiracy theorists blamed the Zika virus on corporate pesticides: "They sprayed pesticides and Zika showed up. Therefore, the pesticides caused Zika." Lacking knowledge, we succumb to fear, make stuff up, find connections where there are none, and hope it's the truth. We want to believe that we have some power over the chaos of our lives.

So Falynn Koch's *Plagues: The Microscopic Battlefield* is just what the doctor ordered. With clarity, humor, and insight, her accessible investigation into the cause and history of plagues provides real power over infectious disease: the power of science. None of this understanding came easily. Plagues killed billions of people before we learned why and how to make them stop. We're still learning. You owe it to yourself and to those died before you to get this invaluable education.

Read. Learn. And wash your hands.

—Bryn Barnard
Author of *Outbreak! Plagues That Changed History*

2

13

By understanding the motivation of plagues, we can work together.

Work together?

HEHEHE

Sure! Germs mutate and change all the time to get better at avoiding or attacking the immune system.

Look at me! Spooky!

Why not mutate for something positive?

ECHO, show what's going on in this room.

HE HE

This technician is observing a showdown between his body's white blood cells and a fast-changing influenza virus.

vmm

vmm

WHoo!

Stand back!

Oooh! Neat!

18

You assaulted the host! You are officially kicked out of the program!

Assaulted?!? I'm the least of your worries!

If this is all a simulation...

...why is everyone so worked up?!

SQUISH

SQUEEEZE

SQUISH

SQUEEEZE

G.RRR

HAHA!

B Cells reporting for duty!

Point out the pathogen and we'll take it from here!

POP!

POP!

29

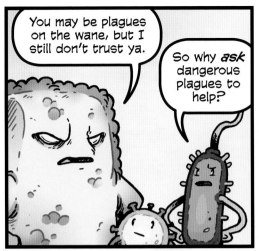

You may be plagues on the wane, but I still don't trust ya.

So why *ask* dangerous plagues to help?

I need a bacterium and a virus, like each of you, for missions.

You both attack cells in unique ways.

You could mutate, with our help, to target the negative things inside humans and be our undercover agents.

But if we're mutated through science...

...will we still be *germs?*

No, you wouldn't.

Germ is a word used to describe any microorganism that makes us sick.

ECHO, please explain.

33

Pasteur did not invent germ theory, but he did prove its validity and use it to make food safer with techniques like pasteurization.

This will kill many harmful bacteria like tuberculosis.

And extend the shelf life of milk.

raw milk

+

heat

Sealed container

Food isn't the only way a bacterium may enter the body and cause sickness.

Unwashed hands that touch the eyes, nose, mouth, or cuts are other routes.

Sick animals can transfer them through biting.

Ahh! While I was picking my nose and eating undercooked meat, this dog bit me!

CHOMP

Since the 1800s, humans have made a point to try to better understand bacteria, in order to prevent illnesses.

We're still learning how many strains of bacteria are out there—there may be too many to count.

But there are a few common types and shapes...

I'm *Borrelia burgdorferi* and my thin corkscrew shape is called a spirochete. I'm famous for causing Lyme disease, which is spread by ticks.

I'm *Campylobacter*. My favorite hiding spot is uncooked poultry. My wide twisty shape is called a spirillum.

I'm *Cholera*, part of the comma-shaped vibrio family, which love moisture. I can be avoided by drinking from clean water sources.

I'm *Streptococcus*. I can cause strep throat and am shaped like a sphere called a coccus. Cocci can be found alone, paired, or clustered.

I'm *Escherichia coli*. I'm a rod-shaped bacillus. I hide in uncooked food and cause intestinal distress when eaten, which is called food poisoning.

Bubonic plague is the most common form of *Yersinia pestis*, the bacteria responsible for the Black Death.

But there are three kinds of deaths that *Yersinia pestis* can cause.

buboni septicemic pneumonic

Many times I spread to the blood stream as well as the lymph nodes.

That's when I'm called *septicemic plague.*

Destroying red blood cells means less oxygen is carried around the body.

RIIIP

RIIIP

RUN!

Without oxygen, fingers, toes, and noses turn black as they rot from the inside out, which is known as gangrene.

I don't look so good.

You look great to me!

Disgusting! In a place this repulsive, a white blood cell can only help so much!

YEEEAH!

Just go anywhere.

In medieval times, there was total ignorance of how disease was spread.

People believed in spontaneous generation and blamed foul-smelling vapors called miasmas.

I've never heard of miasmas before, but they sound great!

Miasmas were noxious smells from rotting trash and waste, also called bad or night air.

People thought you could protect yourself from bad air by shutting windows...

...and smelling pleasant things like incense.

In medieval towns, there was no public sanitation or citywide garbage collection. So there were lots of things to cause stench in the streets.

Soot from chimneys.

Garbage.

No modern bathrooms.

Butchers working outside.

Sick people in the street.

OINK OINK

cluck cluck

Animal manure.

After Louis Pasteur and other scientists proved that bacteria was the cause of sickness, people stopped believing in miasmas altogether.

This allowed for focused attention on the real causes of the Black Death, and bacteria in general.

Alexandre Yersin discovered the plague bacterium in 1894.

It was named after me!

Alexander Fleming discovered penicillin as an antibiotic in 1928.

Pau-Louis Simond proved in 1897 that fleas transmit the bacteria to rats.

A new way to kill bacteria!

Sorry, rats. Bum deal!

Bacteria can adapt and become resistant to antibiotics when they are prescribed for infections that don't need them.

Bacteria can also survive when patients don't finish medication or use it as directed.

Even the antibiotics used in food can pass along antibiotic resistance to the people who eat it!

Antibiotics are only effective in fighting bacteria when used correctly and in moderation.

But thanks to antibiotics, very few people get the plague these days, and they usually recover quickly.

Ugh! This place is so boring now!

The bubonic plagues were terrible, but humans did learn a lot from them.

Crisis can push us to advance our health and science.

All *I'm* hearing is that without *ME*...

...you'd still be pooping on the street and blaming the flu on fart smells!

You may have come a long way, but you'll never get rid of me completely.

Because of that critter right there!

Hi, there!

Boop

SQUEAK

Hey!

vmm vmm vmm vmm SQUEAK!

Ah yes, vectors.

Eliminate *Yersinia pestis!*

Without getting rid of us!

That's enough of the vectors.

Take us back to the body.

Aw!

Yellow, never mind the vectors! Bubonic Plague is a lost cause.

But you still have a choice, Yellow.

But Bub does make some good points!

I used to be a plague too, y'know.

Sure, yellow fever was very scary back when people still believed in miasmas.

But these days, people have learned a lot more about how viruses *actually* work.

The spikes help the virus stick to cells.

Like this!

AHH!

Get off!

SHOVE!

Oh, gross!

There are several shapes of viruses.

I'm the *tobacco mosaic virus*, which affects and kills plants. I'm helical-shaped, like a coiled spring.

I'm *influenza*, a common virus causing the flu. Our spherical shape is usually rough or spiky.

I'm a *polyhedral*, or a gem shape, called an adenovirus. I have large spikes and cause pneumonia in the lungs.

I'm a *bacteriophage*, a complex virus that can infect and replicate inside bacteria. Many of us look alien or robot-like with a multisided "head," a tube "body," and tail fibers or legs.

76

During the warm summer months in coastal cities like Philadelphia...

...mosquitoes flourished and spread the fever quickly.

With no knowledge of vectors, the people in these cities believed they suffered from a miasma plague.

Cough

This was before the research into the science of *immunity,* so experts of the time didn't understand why this fever had little effect on people with dark skin.

People with dark skin in Philadelphia at this time were slaves, or former slaves.

They came from places where yellow fever was common, and had developed an immunity to it as children.

Jenner spent his life trying to eliminate smallpox.

And he led the way to modern routine vaccination.

The "temple of vaccine," as Jenner called it, was a shed in his backyard where he gave free vaccinations to anyone.

After Jenner's death, his work was carried on.

The World Heath Organization eventually eliminated the virus through quarantine and vaccination.

Everything was ruined for me!

TSSST

Ugh! Edward Jenner!

All this "working together"!

The World Health Organization!

"Public health"! *Blech!*

Don't forget, Smallpox, you have no vectors and you only spread through direct contact.

You're saying we're being killed for eating? Something we *have* to do?

Well, you spread lots of terrible plagues.

Bzzz...

Bzzz

So the best way to stop those plagues is to stop *you*.

That's not fair!

Sigh. ECHO, end the mosquito simulation.

vmm

The Panama Canal project was only successful because Gorgas convinced people to believe in vectors and work together.

But what if they hadn't?

Plagues often thrive because people are their *own worst enemies*.

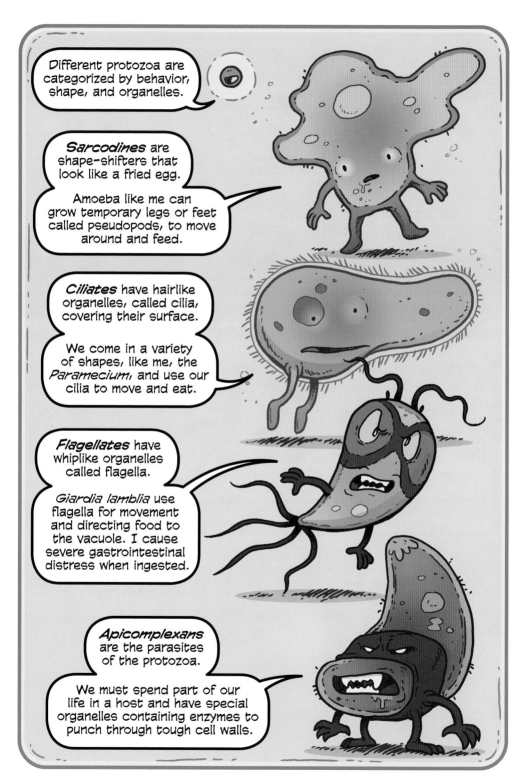

Different protozoa are categorized by behavior, shape, and organelles.

Sarcodines are shape-shifters that look like a fried egg.

Amoeba like me can grow temporary legs or feet called pseudopods, to move around and feed.

Ciliates have hairlike organelles, called cilia, covering their surface.

We come in a variety of shapes, like me, the *Paramecium*, and use our cilia to move and eat.

Flagellates have whiplike organelles called flagella.

Giardia lamblia use flagella for movement and directing food to the vacuole. I cause severe gastrointestinal distress when ingested.

Apicomplexans are the parasites of the protozoa.

We must spend part of our life in a host and have special organelles containing enzymes to punch through tough cell walls.

ECHO, transfer Yellow to the Special Forces team to begin training.

Bye, everyone!

Bye, Bub!

Yeah, yeah.

vmm vmm

Yellow thinks he's happy now...

...but germs and humans aren't supposed to cooperate.

It doesn't have to be that way, you stubborn germ!

I—I'm sorry. I shouldn't yell at you.

ECHO, shut down the—

I can do the job!

I'll prove it!

How?

I already have. There were a bunch of weirdo cells that you missed earlier in the thymus gland.

I tried to tell you.

COUGH

What cells?

Impossible!

There's no way I missed that!

You're trying to weasel your way out of a petri dish!

You think I'm lying?

Whatever they are, T Cell, I'll have them checked out as soon as—

OMPH

Or...Bub, can you take care of those for me right now?

Me?

COUGH

You *can* destroy cells, right?

Of course, but are you sure you want me to...?

Yes. You'd be a *lifesaver*.

ECHO, turn off restrictions for Bubonic Plague.

Elena, no!

It's okay!

I trust him.

Okay, that's all of them!

HA!

TAP

TAP

It looks— *good!*

The real body is responding to the simulated attack.

CLAP CLAP CLAP

Told you I was amazing!

WMP WMP

I have to admit, that was impressive.

Now, *please* tell me you'll join CHAMBER with those skills?

If that's the job, I suppose it *could* be fun.

If you work with us we can make sure *every day* is like that!

Here are some general definitions that are good to know when talking about germs, plagues, and microbiology.

Antibody
Protein produced to counteract a specific antigen. Combines chemically with viruses or substances that the body recognizes as harmful.

Antigen
A toxin or other foreign substance that induces an immune response in the body and the production of antibodies.

Endemic
A disease or condition regularly found among people in a certain area.

Epidemic
A widespread disease in a community during a particular time.

Germ
A microorganism that causes disease.

Immunity
Natural or acquired resistance to a disease using the ability of a white blood cell to react in the presence of an antigen.

Inoculation
Introducing a serum, vaccine, or antigenic substance into the body, to stimulate the production of antibodies or to boost immunity to a specific bacteria, virus, or disease.

Microbe
A microorganism, normally single-celled.

Microorganism
An organism only seen with a microscope and typically only a single cell. Includes bacteria, virus, protozoa, and certain fungi and parasitic worms.

Pandemic
A disease that is spreading in more than one continent at the same time.

Pathogen
An organism causing disease, often a microorganism but also any parasite.

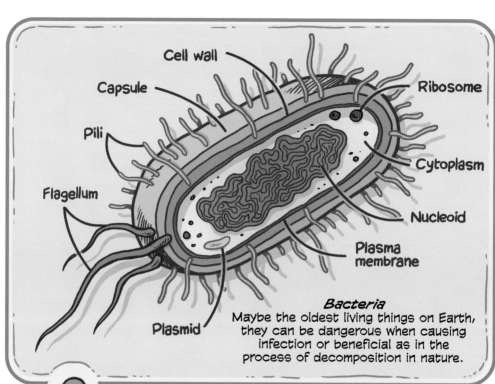

Cell wall
Capsule
Pili
Flagellum
Plasmid
Ribosome
Cytoplasm
Nucleoid
Plasma membrane

Bacteria
Maybe the oldest living things on Earth, they can be dangerous when causing infection or beneficial as in the process of decomposition in nature.

Viruses
The smallest microorganisms, they cannot reproduce or grow without invading a living cell of another organism, causing it harm.

Envelope
Capsid
Genetic material, or genome
Surface studs, or proteins

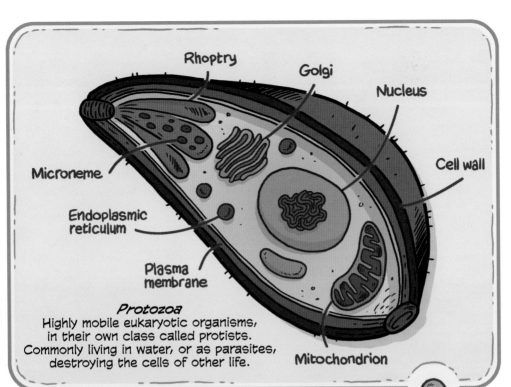

Rhoptry

Golgi

Nucleus

Microneme

Cell wall

Endoplasmic
reticulum

Plasma
membrane

Protozoa
Highly mobile eukaryotic organisms,
in their own class called protists.
Commonly living in water, or as parasites,
destroying the cells of other life.

Mitochondrion

Fungi
A diverse group of single-celled
organisms growing together and
absorbing the organic material
around them in which they live
for energy.

Mitochondrion

Ribosome

Golgi

Cell wall

Plasma
membrane

Cytoplasm

Vacuole

Peroxisome

Periplasm

Endoplasmic
reticulum

Nucleus

These are some important parts of microorganisms that make us what we are!

Cytoplasm
Gel-like substance within the cell membrane that surrounds the organelles.

Endoplasmic reticulum
Provides many functions like metabolism, hormone production, and detoxification.

Eukaryote
Cell containing a nucleus organelle to surround its genetic material.

Flagellum
Whiplike appendage that protrudes from the body of certain cells. Primarily used for movement but also acts as a sensory organelle.

Golgi apparatus
An organelle collecting and dispatching proteins received from the endoplasmic reticulum.

Mitochondrion
The power of the cell, this organelle generates most of the cell's energy.

Nucleoid
An irregularly shaped region within a prokaryotic cell that contains genetic material. It is not surrounded by a membrane.

Nucleus
An organelle in eukaryotic cells that contains genetic material and controls metabolism, growth, and reproduction.

Organelle
Any structure within a eukaryotic cell with its own purpose.

Pili
Hairlike appendage found on the surface of many bacteria that can help exchange genetic material or adhere to other cells.

Prokaryotic
Unicellular microorganism that lacks a nucleus containing genetic material.

I'm Cholera, or *Vibrio cholerae*, and I'm a bacteria living in water. Once ingested, I cause infection of the intestines. Symptoms are severe vomiting and diarrhea, and death by dehydration is common. If I'm reintroduced into drinking water, the process of infection starts over.

I'm Spanish Flu, or Influenza H1N1, a deadly virus that spread quickly after WWI. Other flus like me normally affect children, elderly, and those with weak immune systems, but I infected and killed healthy young adults too. I killed millions in 1918, and unexpectedly disappeared by 1919.

I'm Polio, or Poliomyelitis, a virus affecting the nervous system, causing permanent paralysis or death. Due to fecal-oral transmission, young children not toilet-trained are the most at risk. Immunization can prevent me, but there is no cure. Elimination is possible, as humans are my only carrier.

I'm HIV, the human immunodeficiency virus. The effects I have on the body can never be cured, only controlled with medication. Destroying T cells, I stop the body from fighting infection and eventually lead to AIDS (acquired immune deficiency syndrome). I'm transferred through contact with infected bodily fluids like blood.

Here are some important milestones in the history of learning about and fighting pandemic plague germs.

Black Death bubonic plague spreads from Asia to Europe, killing a quarter of the world population.

Measles is brought by the first foreigners to arrive in Central and South America.

Mary Wortley Montagu inoculates her daughter against smallpox in England, in front of observers.

Yellow fever outbreak in Philadelphia causes panic and death.

Cholera spreads outside India for the first time by British soldiers.

Robert Koch confirms germ theory by identifying anthrax as a bacterium.

Louis Pasteur proves that yeast causes fermentation.

Paul-Louis Simond demonstrates how fleas transmit bubonic plague.

Ronald Ross proves that mosquitoes carry malaria.

The Centers for Disease Control (CDC) is founded.

Spanish flu kills at least 20 million in a year, then disappears.

International panic over polio as the number of children infected and disabled by it climbs.

An unidentified virus (soon to be known as HIV and having originated in Africa in the early 1900s) is discovered in the US and causes panic and the spreading of misinformation.

HIV is indentified and recognized as a pandemic disease.

1347–1351

1531–1534

1721

1793

1816

1857

1876

1897

1918

1946

1952

1970s

1981

120

The first outbreaks of smallpox in the Americas occur from foreign contact.

The Royal Society of London recognizes Antonie van Leeuwenhoek's work in microscopic observations.

Smallpox kills much of the native North, Central, and South American populations due to interaction with Europeans and war.

Edward Jenner successfully vaccinates James Phipps from smallpox.

Pasteur patents the process of pasteurization and disproves spontaneous generation theory with swan neck flask experiments.

John Snow tracks how cholera travels in water as the Broad Street outbreak of London occurs.

Theobald Smith discovers the tick as the first-known vector.

Walter Reed proves that mosquitos spread yellow fever.

Alexander Fleming confirms the antibacterial properties of penicillin.

The World Health Organization (WHO) is founded.

Jonas Salk develops and distributes the first polio vaccines.

The World Health Organization declares that smallpox has been eradicated.

SARS outbreak in China leads international attempt to stop its spread due to air travel.

Largest outbreak of Ebola virus occurs, mostly contained to Africa, but causes panic through world. Quarantine slows and confines its spread.

1519
1673
1775–1782
1796
1854
1864
1893
1900
1929
1948
1955
1980
2002
2014

—NOTES—

Page 37, panel 4
We've been trying to classify living thing into categories since at least the ancient Greeks. The six-kingdom system is the classification system proposed by Simpson and Roger. It is only one of several classification systems. Woese has a three-kingdom sytem, and Simpson and Roger updated their system in 2015 to a seven-kingdom system.

Page 42, panel 2
The second plague pandemic actually ended in the 19th century. It was at its most virulent 1347–51, but reoccured in the centuries thereafter, including the London plagues of 1360–63, the Great Plague of Seville (1647–52), the Great Plague of London (1665–66), the Great Plague of Vienna (1679), the Great Plague of Marseille (1720–22), the Great Plague of 1738, and the Russian plague of 1770–72. It remained a problem in North Africa and the Middle East into the early 1900s.

These are some books that both young and adult readers can enjoy to continue learning about germs, plagues, and their influence on human history as well as individual lives.

—FURTHER READING—

Barnard, Bryn. *Outbreak: Plagues That Changed History*. Dragonfly Books, 2015.

Crawford, Dorothy H. *Deadly Companions: How Microbes Shaped Our History*. Oxford University Press, 2009.

Sachs, Jessica Snyder. *Good Germs, Bad Germs: Health and Survival in a Bacterial World*. Hill and Wang, 2008.

Marrin, Albert. *Dr. Jenner and the Speckled Monster: The Search for the Smallpox Vaccine*. Dutton Juvenile, 2002.

Henderson, D. A. *Smallpox: Death of a Disease*. Prometheus Books, 2009.